DayOne

HELP!

MY SPOUSE HAS
BEEN UNFAITHFUL

Mike Summers

Consulting Editor: Dr. Paul Tautges

© Day One Publications 2010

First printed 2010

ISBN 978-1-84625-220-4

Published by Day One Publications
Ryelands Road, Leominster, HR6 8NZ

TEL 01568 613 740 FAX 01568 611 473

email—sales@dayone.co.uk

UK web site—www.dayone.co.uk

USA web site—www.dayonebookstore.com

Designed by **documen**
Printed by Orchard Press (Cheltenham) Ltd

CONTENTS

Your world has been turned upside down. A future that seemed bright is now clouded by uncertainty and confusion. Your emotions are all over the map. Your thoughts often play imaginary tapes of *them* together. You feel vulnerable and exposed. One moment you feel guilty for hating your spouse because of what happened; the next, you feel guilty for still loving your spouse in light of what happened. You wonder if your years together were just a lie, and you are angry that you didn't see this coming. Tears come uncontrollably and unexpectedly. You feel depressed and alone—even alienated from God. You never dreamed this would happen, but here you are. You are reeling from the news that your spouse has been unfaithful, and you don't know what to do.

The word "affair" does not adequately describe the destruction adultery brings to a marriage. Something belonging only to you has been carelessly given away.

Trust has been shattered and pain has been inflicted. This is something that happens to others, not you—not your marriage! The tsunami of emotions which are experienced when a spouse has been unfaithful can be intense. Betrayal and rejection create within the human heart a sickening unsettledness, and the despair it can create turns life into a lonely journey.

Your friends and family members don't want to see you hurt. Because their primary concern is how you *feel* they take up your offense. Perhaps they tell you things like:

- ▶ "You deserve so much better."
- ▶ "You don't need someone like that in your life."
- ▶ "Life is short. The sooner you can forget about this and move on, the better."
- ▶ "If you stay in this marriage, you know this is only going to happen again."

While they mean well, comments like these only add fuel to your already enflamed emotions and they influence you toward unhelpful responses. You try to filter the advice you receive, but you are not sure where else to turn. Is there any help?

The good news for you is that God provides specific direction for those who have been betrayed, rejected, and wounded by others. The purpose of this booklet is to assist you as you seek to navigate your way through this painful season of your life. The perspective and hope you will find here come from God's Word. What God has to say to you in your crisis is powerful and practical.

You stand at a crossroads, and the decisions you make now will impact the rest of your life. The price of complicating your future, by doing something you may regret later, is high. It is true that your spouse has done something against you that is reprehensible. But consider that your spouse has sinned not only against *you*—but also against God. Therefore, God is involved in this to an even greater extent than you are! Because he knows the hurt you are experiencing and how you got here, he offers you the opportunity to experience his grace in new and fresh ways. In the following pages we will examine what God wants you to do to move forward. He desires to take your hand and walk you into territory you never thought possible. Will you join him?

What Does God Want Me to Do?

To everyone around them, the Johnsons[1] had it made. They seemed to have a storybook marriage and lived what many would consider an enviable life. Ron was a doctor with a thriving practice, and Carol was growing her real-estate business. They had two beautiful children and a large house on a picturesque lake. However, things aren't always as they appear.

When Ron called, his voice lacked its usual confidence and I could immediately tell something terrible had occurred. "Ron, what is it?" I asked. What he said was the last thing I expected to hear. "Mike, I don't know what to do. I just found out that Carol is having an affair." For the next several months Ron and I spoke together on the phone nearly every day. His heart was broken and the pain he experienced was intense.

1   All names have been changed to protect the identity of those involved.

Carol acknowledged to her husband that she was in a relationship with another man and had no intention of cutting it off. Ron was devastated. He begged Carol to stop the relationship so they could work on their marriage. He assured her they could get through this—that their marriage was worth saving. However, with the affair exposed, Carol only became more open and blatant in her new relationship and more callous and hurtful toward Ron. During the day she would stay home with the children, and when Ron came home from work, she would go to her lover's house and return home in the morning. Ron's devastation soon turned to disgust.

His family and friends all counseled him that the marriage was over, since Carol had no desire to return. Ron was advised to protect the kids and file for divorce. He asked, "Mike, what do you think I should do?" I responded, "It doesn't matter what *I* think you should do or what *anyone else* thinks you should do. The real question is, what does *God* want you to do?"

This is the question you must to come to terms with. God's ways are perfect and his counsel is sure. If you are unsure of where you stand right now with God, consider that God has gone to great lengths to demonstrate his love to you. He wants you to turn away from everything else and experience the grace he has made available through his Son.

Even greater than the restoration of a broken marriage is the need for the restoration of a broken life. It may be that God is using your pain to point out your need to be reconciled to him.

The Problem

Adam and Eve had it all: a perfect environment in which to live and a perfect relationship with their Creator. However, through the serpent, doubt was cast on God's goodness. He indicated that God was withholding something precious and they were missing out on all that could be theirs. The couple rejected God in the garden of Eden in order to pursue fulfillment on their own. And through this rebellion against God, sin entered their perfect world. The consequence of this sin would be mankind's separation from God, and death. "Therefore, just as through one man sin entered the world, and death through sin, and thus death spread to all men, because all sinned ..." (Romans 5:12).

Man's greatest problem is that he is a sinner separated from God with a heart and mind that are blinded by sin. Because we are sinners, there is nothing we can do to overcome our sinful condition. Furthermore, because God is righteous and just, it is impossible for him to overlook and excuse our sin. To do so would violate who he is as God. God's justice must be satisfied and our sin must be punished. Nothing short of this satisfies God's righteousness. But God is not only righteous and just, he is also merciful and loving.

The Solution

God extended grace to man by promising to send a Redeemer who would reconcile his rebellious enemies to himself. For centuries people waited for God's Redeemer to come. Finally, God's Son was sent as the only solution for man's problem. However, when he came, he was rejected. "He came to His own, and His own did not receive Him" (John 1:11).

Jesus's life had shone brightly as the light of the world, but those in darkness hated the light and would not come to the light. The very one God sent was willfully rejected, spitefully betrayed, shamefully abused, and violently put to death. However, as Jesus was dying on the cross, the very purpose of God was unfolding. Sin demands the full fury of God's wrath to be leveled against it. And in obedience to the Father's plan, Jesus took our sin, requiring God the Father to pour out his wrath upon his own Son! On the cross, Jesus became a substitute for sinners, providing atonement for the sins of everyone who would ever believe. Jesus's sacrificial death completely satisfied God's righteous demands, enabling him to forgive and declare righteous all who come to him by faith. "For He [God the Father] made Him who knew no sin [God the Son] to be sin for us, that we might become the righteousness of God in Him" (2 Corinthians 5:21).

The good news for sinners like you and me is that by embracing God's Son by faith and entrusting him with our lives, we can have peace with God! Through this "new birth," God offers us new life. "Therefore, if anyone is in Christ, he is a new creation; old things have passed away; behold, all things have become new" (2 Corinthians 5:17).

If you have never received Jesus Christ as Lord and Savior, turn to him today. Ask God to open your eyes to the weight of sin you are carrying, throw yourself upon the mercy of God, and cry out to him to save you.

First Steps

While you did not sign up for this when you got married, the reality is that you are here and you cannot go back and undo what has happened—you must move forward. However, to move forward in the right direction you need to be sure you are taking the right action. The journey ahead will not be easy. At times you may even find it to be excruciatingly difficult. Following the steps outlined in this chapter is no guarantee that your marriage will be restored, but if you choose to follow them you will find your relationship with God will become richer than you ever thought possible.

Ron was a believer in Christ, but over the years his spiritual life had become cold and stale. He was seeking fulfillment not in Christ, but in his career, in things, and in his notoriety as a prominent member of his community. As a result, his walk with Christ had lost intensity and passion. This showed up in his life personally and in his home. Ron went to church but it was mainly for social purposes. He seldom read Scripture and when he prayed, it was void of any sense of urgency. At home he failed to fulfill his responsibilities as a spiritual leader and most evenings were spent detached from his family, watching television until he fell asleep.

The news that Carol was in a relationship with another man shook the very foundations on which Ron was building his life. In his time of crisis the things he had considered so important had no value. He had wasted years pursuing what didn't matter, and now what *did* matter was coming apart. What Ron needed to do was turn his attention away from everything else and put it back on God.

Turn Your Attention to God

What God does is always right because he is righteous (just and holy). His work and ways are always perfect in every way. What you know and believe about God will be what enables you to do what he wants. As you face trouble you can be confident that you have a God who is near. This means that, while you may feel alone, you are not alone. All believers in Christ have the guarantee of God's continued presence, for he promised, "I will never leave you nor forsake you." And because of this, even in adversity we can boldly say, "The Lord is my helper; I will not fear; what can man do to me?" (Hebrews 13:5–6).

It is important for you to realize that not only is your spouse accountable to God for his or her actions, so too are you. What will you do? Your choices are limited: you can depend on your own strength and try to face this alone, or you can depend on the unlimited power of God and rest in him.

God has an amazing purpose to accomplish in your life regardless of how your spouse responds. Sometimes while in the throes of pain we are unable to see any purpose for what we are experiencing. To think that God would allow pain into our lives seems inconceivable. But God is always good and his purposes are always good. In his faithfulness he may take us through undesirable pain, but he will never allow us to experience unbearable pain.

No temptation has overtaken you except such as is common to man; but God is faithful, who will not allow you to be tempted beyond what you are able, but with the temptation will also make the way of escape, that you may be able to bear it.

(1 Corinthians 10:13)

Joseph was a young man who was betrayed, abused, and sold into slavery by members of his own family. As a slave he was taken to a foreign country, accused of a heinous crime, and thrown into prison, where he was forgotten for several years. Yet through the rejection and all of the pain, Joseph's attention was riveted on God. Years later he stood before his family members who had hurt him so deeply and announced his confidence in God:

But as for you, you meant evil against me;
but God meant it for good, in order to
bring it about as it is this day, to save many
people alive.

(Genesis 50:20)

God can be trusted. He is both sovereign and good. He causes what others intend as evil to be used for his good purposes.

And we know that all things work together
for good to those who love God, to those
who are the called according to His

purpose. For whom He foreknew, He also
predestined to be conformed to the image
of His Son, that He might be the firstborn
among many brethren.

(Romans 8:28–29)

This means that God causes *all* things—things that
are good, pleasant, and easy, as well as things that are
disappointing, painful, and hard—to work together
to accomplish his purpose in those who belong
to him.

Perhaps you consider your greatest need right now
to be to *feel* better or for your marriage to get "fixed."
These are great needs, to be sure, but your greatest
need is for God. Look to him. Trust him. Commit
to putting God above everything and anyone else,
and follow him regardless of where he may take
you. He is your only hope. "Whom have I in heaven
but You? And there is none upon earth that I desire
besides You. My flesh and my heart fail; but God is
the strength of my heart and my portion forever"
(Psalm 73:25–26).

Those who seek to follow God are not immune
from rejection and betrayal. In Psalm 42 the psalmist
freely exposed the anguish of his heart as he was
going through a time of great difficulty. What he

recorded is raw and intense. Notice how he vividly described what he felt: "As the deer pants for the water brooks, so pants my soul for You, O God. My soul thirsts for God, for the living God. When shall I come and appear before God?" (vv. 1–2). When a deer in the wilderness needs water, it will begin its search with eager anticipation. However, when no water is found, the dehydrated deer will panic, become disoriented, and in a frenzied state will run itself to death. The psalmist laments that, in the same way, he longs for God, because in his distress he feels alone. He is desperate for God.

When we feel crushed it becomes an opportunity for God to become our greatest pursuit. Pouring out to God how we feel gives voice to our pain. It enables us to take what concerns us most and give it to the One who cares the most for us.

> *Therefore humble yourselves under the mighty hand of God, that He may exalt you in due time, casting all your care upon Him, for He cares for you.*
>
> (1 Peter 5:6–7)

Ignoring pain does not make it better. You may think that distancing yourself from a spouse who has hurt you so deeply will help you deal with the pain, but it won't. If you do not honestly confront the pain that has come into your life and give it to God, you may eventually turn to self-destructive means to deal with it.

For the psalmist, the pain of rejection and betrayal left him feeling emotionally shattered. He lost his appetite and spent most of his time in tears. His situation felt hopeless, but he didn't hesitate to express this reality to God: "My tears have been my food day and night, while they continually say to me, 'Where is your God?'" (v. 3). He realized that emotionally he was a wreck. However, rather than give in to how he felt, he fought for perspective. He chose to view his circumstances through God's character rather than interpret God's character through his circumstances. This led him to look to God through his tears. While his tears were saying, "Where is your God?" he guided his heart to hope in God:

> When I remember these things,
> I pour out my soul within me.
> For I used to go with the multitude;
> I went with them to the house of God,
> With the voice of joy and praise,

With a multitude that kept a pilgrim feast.
Why are you cast down, O my soul?
And why are you disquieted within me?
Hope in God, for I shall yet praise Him
For the help of His countenance.

(vv. 4–5)

God is your greatest need. Fight for perspective and look to him. Recall how you have experienced God's faithfulness in the past and praise him for the help he will provide you now. Resolve to look beyond yourself and intentionally seek a God *who is here*. Don't wait to turn your heart to him when you think it will be easier—look to him *now* because he is your only hope!

Identify Your Personal Issues

Those who learn that a spouse has been unfaithful experience a wide spectrum of emotions and responses. For Ron, the rejection and betrayal left him devastated and plagued by feelings of guilt. He wondered what he had done that could cause Carol to choose someone else over him. He pleaded and begged her to love him, vowing to change whatever it was that she didn't like. However, Ron's groveling only caused Carol to become more distant and detached from him.

Ron was trying to manipulate Carol and it didn't work. Because Ron's focus was on himself and not God, his initial emotional responses gave way to more lethal responses. Disgust, anger, and feelings of revenge found clever ways to inflict pain on Carol through his careless self-oriented words and actions. She had hurt him deeply and he felt she needed to pay for it. He wanted to see her feel the pain he felt. There came a point when he doubted he could ever love her again and was so eaten up with bitterness that he wanted to give up and file for divorce.

WHAT HAS BEEN YOUR RESPONSE?

When we have been sinned against, the temptation to return evil for evil can be strong. Scripture, however, instructs believers to leave justice in the hands of God:

> Repay no one evil for evil. Have regard for
> good things in the sight of all men. If it is
> possible, as much as depends on you, live
> peaceably with all men. Beloved, do not
> avenge yourselves, but rather give place to
> wrath; for it is written, "Vengeance is Mine, I
> will repay," says the Lord. (Romans 12:17–19)

Bitterness is a noxious weed that infects the heart and mind. If it is allowed to live, other sins begin to move in, take over, and overwhelm the bitter person:

> Pursue peace with all people, and holiness, without which no one will see the Lord: looking carefully lest anyone fall short of the grace of God; lest any root of bitterness springing up cause trouble, and by this many become defiled.
>
> (Hebrews 12:14–15)

There are thee ways that bitterness is like a root. First, bitterness grows beneath the surface in the heart and may not be detected until it sprouts. Weeds typically aren't detected until the environment is right. The bright yellow flower of a dandelion which appears in April reveals that the weed took root the previous summer. In the same way, the root of bitterness may not be detected until its "flower" blooms.

Second, bitterness becomes the source of other problems that become manifest in our lives. If a dandelion is left alone, its seeds will spread and produce other weeds after its kind. In the same way, if allowed to continue, bitterness creates a host of additional unwanted problems in our lives.

Third, bitterness has the potential to create trouble and defile others. Bitterness is not something that appears out of nowhere. The seeds of bitterness begin small and then develop into a destructive root. The soil in which bitterness grows becomes fertile through a relational wound left unresolved. This wound becomes the poisoned soil from which the root of bitterness develops. A grudge is nurtured, feelings of animosity begin to emerge, and a critical spirit takes over. The bitter person ultimately insists he or she has a *right* to feel this way.

Feelings of bitterness are at the very heart of revenge, hatred, anger, and a host of other sinful behaviors that deaden us spiritually. Unresolved bitterness can greatly hinder what God wants to do in your life. There are six deadly effects of responding to unwanted pain with bitterness:

1. *Bitterness disrupts peace.* Bitterness creates turmoil in our lives. It causes anxiety and disturbs the peace of God that is to guard our hearts.

2. *Bitterness destroys joy.* Bitterness has the potential to destroy the joy in your life, your

23

family, and your relationships with others, and will manifest itself in hurtful and harmful ways throughout the course of your life.

3. *Bitterness depletes strength.* The root of bitterness sucks the life-giving nutrients from the soil of our lives that we need to stand firm. Bitterness must be nurtured to survive, and a bitter person spends a vast amount of energy keeping the weed alive—energy that should be expended on spiritual pursuits and healthy relationships. Bitterness hardens our hearts and opens the door to other sins.

4. *Bitterness distorts focus.* Bitterness views life through a distorted lens that twists reality and blinds us to our own faults. It causes us to shift our focus from the Lord and place it on ourselves and the pain we feel. Bitterness prevents us from seeing how God can use what we experience for our good.

5. *Bitterness defiles relationships.* Bitterness stems from an unforgiving spirit. People who are bitter are typically harsh, critical, and judgmental toward others. But it does not always show up in such aggressive ways. It may manifest itself as

indifference, self-pity, or callousness. Bitterness leads us to distance ourselves from those with whom we are bitter. We *want* them to hurt because in our bitterness we believe they *deserve* to hurt.

6. *Bitterness displeases God*. When we live with unresolved bitterness, we become prisoners of our own making. Bitterness takes us down a spiral of discouragement, depression, and despair. When we choose to hold on to a grudge, we end up inflicting more injury to ourselves than to anyone else. You cannot minimize the sin by claiming, "I'm not bitter—I'm just deeply hurt." Do not excuse the sin of bitterness. By confessing bitterness as a sin against God, you accept responsibility for your response to the pain in your life.

All sin is an affront to a holy God—no matter how "justified" we may believe that sin to be. It is imperative that you guard against assuming a self-righteous posture that reasons, "At least *my* sin isn't adultery!" Just because you haven't been unfaithful, it doesn't mean there is nothing for which you are culpable. Just as God hates the adultery of your spouse, so he also hates the sins which may have crept into your life.

WHERE ARE YOU FAILING?

If the adulterer is your wife, God's commands to you now are no different from those to you before her adultery. You are still to:

▸ love her as Christ loves the church
  (Ephesians 5:25)

▸ extend to her understanding and honor
  (1 Peter 3:7)

▸ not become embittered against her
  (Colossians 3:19).

If the adulterer is your husband, God's commands to you now are also no different from those to you before his adultery. You are still to:

▸ show him honor and respect (Ephesians 5:33)

▸ respond to his leadership and authority
  (1 Peter 3:1–6).

This cuts against the grain of what seems to be natural. Rather than protect yourself, God wants you to humble yourself and confront your personal failures.

Deal Honestly With Your Sins

God wants your heart to be clean. If your desire is to follow God, then you must acknowledge your sins and experience his forgiveness (see "Personal Application Project 2: Getting Things Right with God," at the end of this booklet). Confessing your sins honestly to God will take you from the burden of sin's oppressive weight to the blessing of God's freeing forgiveness.

> *Blessed is he whose transgression is forgiven,*
> *Whose sin is covered ...*
> *When I kept silent, my bones grew old*
> *Through my groaning all the day long.*
> *For day and night Your hand was heavy*
>   *upon me ...*
> *I acknowledged my sin to You ...*
> *I said, "I will confess my transgressions to*
>   *the Lord,"*
> *And You forgave the iniquity of my sin.*
>   *(Psalm 32:1–5)*

WHAT IF I DON'T FEEL FORGIVEN?

Some wrongly assume that, because they don't *feel* forgiven, they aren't forgiven. But the fact of God's forgiveness cannot be based on how we feel. The Bible teaches that when we confess our sins, God forgives our sins. If we are forgiven by God, we are forgiven—period.

Some who are forgiven may not feel forgiven because they still struggle with temptation. God's forgiveness of sin doesn't remove the temptation to sin. Temptation is not sin; giving in to temptation is. When we do yield to temptation, we must again come to God in confession and experience his cleansing.

Others who are forgiven may not feel forgiven because they are experiencing some of the fallout of their sinful behavior. God's forgiveness of sin doesn't remove the consequences of sin.

The feelings of being forgiven by God are experienced when we *believe* that we are forgiven by God. The blessing of being forgiven by God is liberating. Sin grieves and quenches the Holy Spirit's work in our lives. Unconfessed sin hardens the heart and numbs the conscience, causing us to become callous, cold, and critical. However, God's cleansing of sin restores our hearts to spiritual vitality, enabling us to express joy, grace, love, and compassion.

What's Next?

When Ron recognized how marginalizing the Lord had grieved God's Spirit and hurt his family, he began to pour out his heart to God. He began by asking God to forgive him for seeking other things to bring fulfillment. He confessed the sins of his heart, mind, words, and actions which had all become a spiritual barrier in his life. He acknowledged how he had lashed out at Carol and slandered her to others, and how anger and bitterness had infected his heart.

As Ron cried out to God he could feel the weight of sin lifted from his heart. He sensed God's presence again and through the tears he found himself praising God for being so good and gracious to him. Then Ron found himself uttering these words from the depths of his heart: "Lord, Carol has wounded me deeply and I feel so betrayed. She is leaving me for someone else and it hurts. But you have forgiven me for so much! You have taken all my sin and nailed it to the cross. And because of that, I forgive Carol. Lord, I release her from this. I cannot carry it any longer. I want to love her and to express your grace to her. Please help me get out of the way so that you can work on her heart."

Ron discovered that there is freedom in forgiveness. Because he was forgiven, he was therefore able to forgive. The fact is, what your spouse has done against you and God may be inexcusable, but it is not unforgivable. God calls you to forgive.

Forgiveness honestly acknowledges that there has been an offense against us for which another is responsible, and then releases the offender to God on the basis of his forgiveness of us. When you forgive:

- you become free to see how God uses what is painful for your ultimate good;

- you become free to appreciate how much you have been forgiven by God;

- you are free to move forward.

One reason people hesitate to forgive is because of a fear that, "If I forgive, they'll be getting away with what they did!" Unforgiveness deceives us into thinking that, if we forgive, justice will not be done, so we are tempted to keep the offense alive in our hearts. But rather than nurture a spirit of unforgiveness in your heart, God wants you to replace it by extending forgiveness from your heart:

> And do not grieve the Holy Spirit of God,
> by whom you were sealed for the day of
> redemption. Let all bitterness, wrath,
> anger, clamor, and evil speaking be put
> away from you, with all malice. And
> be kind to one another, tenderhearted,
> forgiving one another, even as God in
> Christ forgave you.
>
> (Ephesians 4:30–32)

We are commanded to forgive others even as God has forgiven us. We are not to forgive others because they *deserve* to be forgiven—your spouse doesn't deserve your forgiveness any more than you deserve God's forgiveness. We are to forgive because God commands us to. Refusing to forgive is an act of defiance against him. What God calls you to do, he enables you to do. And he wants you to be gripped by your need to forgive.

A Lesson on Forgiveness

In the technical sense, forgiveness is the cancellation of a debt that frees the debtor from all liability to pay. To understand how we are to forgive others, we must understand and appreciate how completely we have been forgiven by God. It is God's forgiveness of us that serves as the basis for how we are to forgive others.

After teaching on how to secure spiritual restoration when one person has sinned against another, Jesus was approached by Peter, who asked him a very practical question about forgiveness: "How many times should I forgive?" In response, Jesus told a story about a king and two of his servants in Matthew 18:23–35.

This king desired to settle accounts with his servants. One servant was brought to the king who owed him 10,000 talents—an unbelievable amount of money. *One* talent was worth 6,000 denarii, and one denarius was considered a fair wage for one day's work. So one talent was about seventeen years' worth of wages for one man—yet the debt owed the king was 10,000 talents! This was equal to seventeen years' worth of wages for 10,000 men! In today's terms, if the average yearly income for one man is $50,000, the debt owed the king would be the equivalent of $8.5 billion! Jesus's point was that the debt owed the king was staggering.

The servant was unable to pay the huge debt he owed. His inability to pay required that he, along with his family and all of his assets, be sold and the proceeds of that sale applied to the debt. The helpless debtor fell in desperation before the king and begged for more time to pay his debt.

The king demonstrated a great measure of grace to the servant and completely forgave the enormous debt. The king himself would absorb the loss and cover the debt. This picture reflects our helpless position before God as sinners. We had a sin debt toward God that was impossible to ever pay, but God paid the debt in full through the death of his Son, thereby releasing us from all liability to pay.

The forgiven servant in the story then went and found a fellow servant who owed him a debt of 100 denarii. This amount in today's terms is the equivalent of just under $13,000. The debt was legitimately owed but it was a mere fraction of the $8.5 billion that had been forgiven. Yet the forgiven servant's posture toward his debtor was harsh and brutal. He laid his hands on him, took him by the throat, and demanded payment immediately.

The servant with the lesser debt made the same appeal made by the servant with the greater debt: he fell before the servant and pleaded for grace. However, rather than extend grace, the servant who had experienced mercy from the king demanded justice and threw his debtor into prison. This response from one who had been shown such mercy grieved the other servants and compelled them to report what had occurred to the king.

The king was outraged. He described the unforgiving servant as "wicked" and charged him with being merciless. The king was furious that he had shown no compassion, no pity and no grace—there was only justice. Since justice was what the unmerciful servant required from his debtor, the king showed the unforgiving servant justice too, and turned him over to the torturers until he paid all that he owed.

What Was Jesus's Point?

Jesus concluded his story by stressing God's heart about unforgiveness. Since God has forgiven us an insurmountable debt of sin against him, he requires us to forgive others their lesser sin debts against us:

> *So My heavenly Father also will do to you if*

each of you, from his heart, does not forgive
his brother his trespasses.

(v. 35)

Jesus's point in this story couldn't be clearer:
God has shown grace and mercy to us by forgiving
our sins against him; therefore we must show grace
and mercy to others by forgiving them their sins
against us.

Two Levels of Forgiveness

The Bible speaks of forgiveness at two levels. One
level is unconditional, nonverbal, and internal,
requiring us to forgive another regardless of whether
that person asks to be forgiven or not. The other is
conditional, verbal, and external, requiring us to
extend forgiveness when it is sought.

UNCONDITIONAL FORGIVENESS
Unconditional forgiveness is an action taken internally
in your heart between you and God in which you
release another person from a sin debt against you,
regardless of whether there is repentance. This kind
of unconditional forgiveness is based on grace—not
on how our offender has responded:

> *And whenever you stand praying, if you*
> *have anything against anyone, forgive him,*
> *that your Father in heaven may also forgive*
> *you your trespasses. But if you do not*
> *forgive, neither will your Father in heaven*
> *forgive your trespasses.*
>
> (Mark 11:25–26)

This indicates that you cannot wait to forgive until your spouse repents of adultery and asks you for forgiveness. Unconditional forgiveness releases your spouse to God in your heart and chooses not to hold the sin against him or her. While unconditional forgiveness releases your spouse from the sin against you, it does not grant forgiveness for the sin against God. Your spouse is still accountable to God, who alone can forgive sins against him.

Unconditional forgiveness is a deliberate choice based on love for and obedience to God. As we have seen, Ephesians 4:32 reveals that we are to forgive in the same way God forgave us: "And be kind to one another, tenderhearted, forgiving one another, even as God in Christ forgave you." "Forgiving ... even as God ... forgave you" indicates at least four characteristics that are to be present in your forgiveness:

1. *You are to forgive obediently.* Since you are commanded to forgive, the motivation for forgiving your spouse is a desire to honor and please God. It was Jesus's obedience that enabled God's forgiveness. In the garden of Gethsemane before his crucifixion, Jesus asked the Father if there was any other way to forgive sinners than his having to experience the cup of God's wrath: "Father, if it is Your will, take this cup away from Me; nevertheless not My will, but Yours, be done" (Luke 22:42). Jesus knew the only way to secure forgiveness for sinners was for him to drink every drop of God's wrath against their sin. As dreadful as this was, he willingly submitted to the Father's will and, as a result, all believers in Christ have been graciously forgiven.

2. *You are to forgive sacrificially.* Forgiveness is not cheap—it costs! To be forgiven by God, it required unimaginable pain and suffering for his Son. Likewise, when you forgive from your heart you relinquish your "right" to hold on to your spouse's sin against you. By forgiving your spouse in your heart, you choose to extend grace, mercy, and love, regardless of what action they take.

37

3. *You are to forgive completely*. There is no such thing as *partial forgiveness*. God did not grant you forgiveness on the installment plan—it was total and complete. If you are a Christian, your entire sin debt against him was paid in full. When you forgive your spouse, you are doing the same. You are in essence making a twofold promise.

First, you are promising not to remember this sin against your spouse again. This is not a promise to "forgive and forget." An omniscient (all-knowing) God cannot "forget" what we have done; rather he chooses *not to remember* our sin against us: "For I will forgive their iniquity, and their sin I will remember no more" (Jeremiah 31:34). It may be possible to forget something as insignificant as where you put your keys, but it is *not* possible to forget something as significant as infidelity! When you forgive your spouse from your heart you are not forgetting, but you are committing to relinquish your ownership of your spouse's sin and give it over to God. By promising before God not to remember this sin against your spouse ever again, you are committing to not bring up the offense again in your mind in order to brood over it or dwell on it.

38

Second, you are promising not to use this sin against your spouse again. This is a commitment to never bring the sin up through your words to your spouse. This does *not* mean that the two of you will never speak of it again (you will need to discuss it if you both choose to work on your marriage), but that you will never use this infidelity as a weapon against your spouse in the future. You are committing to not use this as slander or gossip about him or her, and to not bring reproach or shame upon him or her by airing it among others.

4. *You are to forgive continuously*. Forgiveness is an action in your heart that is ongoing. The Greek participle translated "forgiving" in Ephesians 4:32 indicates ongoing action. Because forgiveness is continual, it may require going to God repeatedly to release your offender from the same offense.

Conditional Forgiveness

This second level is forgiveness expressed to your spouse *after* he or she repents from the sin and asks for forgiveness. Conditional forgiveness can only be expressed if unconditional forgiveness has already occurred in the heart:

39

> *Take heed to yourselves. If your brother sins*
> *against you, rebuke him; and if he repents,*
> *forgive him. And if he sins against you*
> *seven times in a day, and seven times in a*
> *day returns to you, saying, "I repent," you*
> *shall forgive him.*
>
> (Luke 17:3–4)

If your spouse has repented from his or her infidelity and asked you for forgiveness, you must forgive your spouse in your heart and then express your forgiveness verbally from your heart.

The unfaithfulness of your spouse may have left you burned, scared, and bitter, but you cannot allow yourself to hold on to his or her sin. Doing so only keeps you bound to what happened in the past. You must surrender all this to God and forgive your spouse.

From his heart, Ron had forgiven Carol. Through forgiveness he found his heart redirected toward his wife. He looked for ways to demonstrate love and grace to her even while she was being so cold and hateful to him in her actions and through her words. She filed for divorce and demanded custody of the children. However, rather than retaliate in kind, Ron sought to live out Jesus's instructions on how to respond toward those who hate, curse, and use you:

> But I say to you who hear: Love your
> enemies, do good to those who hate you,
> bless those who curse you, and pray for
> those who spitefully use you.
>
> (Luke 6:27–28)

Ron looked for ways in which he could demonstrate love to Carol and made it his aim to serve her. He became reengaged with his children by caring for their needs and he tried to be helpful to Carol by cleaning the house, doing the laundry, and preparing meals. The more Ron served his unrepentant wife, the more his love for her grew. He prayed for Carol's heart to be turned to God and to be broken over her sin, and for their marriage to be restored.

Ron daily repeated his love and commitment to Carol. He reminded her frequently that what she was doing was sin against God and that she would never find fulfillment without Christ being first in her life. One day, however, Ron's love and commitment to restoring his marriage was stretched to the limit. Carol said to him, "Ron, it's too late. You need to forget about me. It can never work. I am two months pregnant." This was another devastating blow that nearly destroyed Ron. He immediately went to God and poured out his heart. Could he continue? Would he be able to love and be father to a child that came from his wife's adultery? Was God's grace sufficient for *that*? The next day, Ron told Carol he was confident that God would provide him with the grace necessary to love her and the baby, and that he was still committed to her.

Six weeks later, as Ron was leaving church with his two children, Carol met him at the car. "Ron, I know that I have been living in sin. I have sinned against God and against you as my husband. Everything about my life is wrong. I don't love you right now, but I know that because God wants our marriage to work, he will restore my heart for you. I have broken off my sinful relationship and have asked God to forgive me. Now I'm asking you: Ron, will you please forgive me?"

Because Ron had already forgiven Carol in his heart, he was free to express his forgiveness to his repentant wife. Ron and Carol sought help together through a biblical counselor to rebuild their marriage, and Carol received help in dealing with issues that had been unaddressed for years. Sixteen years later, the Johnsons are still a vivid testimony of the power and grace of God.

What if My Spouse Continues the Infidelity?

Many marriages that have experienced the horror and betrayal of adultery are restored. However, many are not because sometimes the unfaithful spouse continues in the infidelity. If this is your experience, you will need to rely on the abundant and all-sufficient grace of God that is extended in times such as these. He will sustain, help, and comfort you in ways that are appropriate to your specific needs. Are there some steps you can take toward reconciliation with your unrepentant spouse? What must you do if your spouse continues in the infidelity?

1. *Forgive your spouse unconditionally.* This is something that must be done before any other action should be considered. As we have seen, your heart needs to be free from any bitterness,

resentment, hatred, or malice before you can proceed further.

2. *Confront your spouse about the sin.* Your spouse needs to understand that the adultery is a sin against God and against you. Jesus states that since you are the one who is aware of the sin, you are the one who is responsible to confront it:

> Moreover if your brother sins against you, go and tell him his fault between you and him alone. If he hears you, you have gained your brother. (Matthew 18:15)

This confrontation is to be done by you *alone* and not by committee. If your spouse acknowledges the sin, repents, and asks you for forgiveness, you must extend forgiveness. If this happens, "you have gained your brother." However, if your spouse does not respond to your confrontation and continues in the relationship, you are to return and confront your spouse along with one or two others:

> But if he will not hear, take with you one or two more, that "by the mouth of

two or three witnesses every word may
be established."   (Matthew 18:16)

The purpose of bringing one or two others is to
preserve the integrity of the restoration process.
It brings additional pressure to bear upon your
spouse as others are brought into the knowledge
of the sin, and it ensures that your spouse has
been confronted and given the opportunity to
repent. If your spouse is still unresponsive and
continues in the relationship, you are to take an
additional step.

3. *Involve your church in the process.* The context
for spiritual restoration is the church. If you
are part of a Bible-believing church, God has
provided you with a valuable resource for
restoring a spouse who is in unrepentant sin:

And if he refuses to hear them, tell it to
the church.

                    (Matthew 18:17)

At this point in the process, the circle of
knowledge about the adultery is enlarged to
include the entire community of believers to
whom you and your spouse are accountable. You

45

should speak with the leaders of your church and inform them that you have taken the steps as outlined above and would like to involve your church in the process of restoring your spouse.

The spiritual leaders of your church are responsible for bringing the matter to the entire congregation, asking each person to engage in the loving confrontation of your spouse. "Telling it to the church" is not intended to drive your spouse away but rather to bring added pressure to bear, moving your spouse toward repentance. It releases your church family to pursue a brother or sister in sin and urge him or her to repent and return to fellowship with God and with them.

If your spouse turns to God after being pursued by the church, the repentance should be made known publicly (just as the *sin* was made known publicly). No further action is needed. However, if your sinning spouse "refuses even to hear the church" (Matthew 18:17), then additional pressure must be brought to bear:

... if he refuses even to hear the church,
let him be to you like a heathen and a
tax collector. (Matthew 18:17)

46

Unrepentant, hard-hearted, persistent sin exposes the potential of an unregenerate heart. The church's pursuit of your spouse at this point in the process is to be with the gospel. Jesus's approach toward the heathen and tax collectors in the Gospels was always with grace by which he pursued them with the hope of the gospel.

In the same way that an unbeliever is not a member of the body of Christ, an unrepentant sinner who has refused to hear the church cannot continue as a member of that church. He or she is to be set apart from the rest of the body as an unbeliever who needs Christ.

The goal of this step is no different from that for the previous steps—it is restoration. If at any point in the process your spouse cuts off the adultery, turns to God in repentance, and asks you for forgiveness, there must be a full restoration with you and the church.

4. *Wait on God.* Don't close the door to reconciliation with your spouse. Even if your spouse divorces you, it is not too late. Restoration becomes impossible *only* if your spouse remarries. If your spouse persists in a life of sin, God will give you

courage to wait as you continue to look to him.

This is a time for you to experience God's faithfulness. Approach him with a teachable spirit that is eager to wait on him. God does have a future for you and he will lead you—don't lose heart:

Wait on the LORD;
Be of good courage,
And He shall strengthen your heart;
Wait, I say, on the LORD!

(Psalm 27:14)

CONCLUSION

Where do you go from here? If your spouse has been unfaithful, you likely identify with one of the following three scenarios:

1. *Your spouse has repented, asked you for forgiveness, and you have forgiven him or her in your heart before God and expressed that forgiveness to your spouse.* If this describes you then you are at a great place to rebuild your marriage. The two of you would be wise at this point to address the issues that were present in your marriage *prior* to the adultery. Major life-altering sins never occur in a vacuum; typically present are other issues which create the unhealthy environment for these sinful choices.

As a couple, work together to change that environment so that old patterns and habits can be replaced with new, God-honoring ones. If you need help with this, seek the assistance of a pastor, biblical counselor, or mature believer who has experience in helping couples build strong marriages.

2. *Your spouse has repented and asked you for forgiveness, but you haven't yet forgiven him or her.* If this describes you, you cannot allow your bitterness and unforgiveness to destroy your life and drive your spouse away in despair. Your unforgiveness poises your life to spiral further away from God into self-pity, depression, and self-destructive choices. You must begin to view your refusal to forgive as sin against God. Your spouse has repented from the sin and *you* are now the one in rebellion—it is *you* who must now repent from sin and turn to God.

    If you need someone to help you work through the issues in your life, contact a pastor or biblical counselor immediately. Do not wait any longer. Time cannot heal what you are experiencing— only God can.

3. *Your spouse is unrepentant and has given no indication of breaking off the sinful relationship. However, you have forgiven your spouse in your*

heart and are waiting for him or her to repent.
If this describes you, you are experiencing the
painful and lonely journey of ongoing rejection.
However, you are also positioned to experience
God's grace, comfort, and compassion in ways
you otherwise would not.

If you have not yet gone through the process of
restoration provided through church discipline
(given in Matthew 18:15–17), speak with your
pastor or elder at your church. Ask if they
practice the process that Jesus outlined. If they
do, then initiate that process.

If you are not a member of a church, you should
still go to your spouse alone and confront him
or her about the sin that has been committed
against you and God. If there is no repentance,
bring one or two mature believers and confront
your spouse again. This requires a spirit of
gentleness. Galatians 6:1 states,

Brethren, if a man is overtaken in any
trespass, you who are spiritual restore such
a one in a spirit of gentleness, considering
yourself lest you also be tempted.

Look for ways to fulfill your responsibilities to your spouse as a husband or wife. If your spouse has moved out of the house, this will be difficult, but keep the door of reconciliation open and continue to pray for your spouse to turn to God. Your hope must remain in God with the resolve that, even if your spouse never comes back, you will continue to pursue God with your whole heart.

God hates sin—all sin. But he has provided forgiveness for sinners through Jesus's finished work on the cross. Because of that, we can be forgiven. And when we experience the freedom that comes from his forgiveness, we are able to forgive. That is the help God provides for those whose spouses have been unfaithful.

Personal Application Projects

Project 1:
Identifying Emotional Responses

Emotional responses to trouble can be overwhelming. Feelings can capture our minds, impede our progress, rob our peace, destroy our joy, devastate our confidence, and negatively impact our choices.

1. Check the emotions you have experienced since discovering your spouse's adultery (see table overleaf).

2. Write down any other emotions that may have surfaced in your life.

3. Why is it unwise to follow your heart? Read Proverbs 4:23. What instruction are you given concerning your heart? According to this verse, why is this important? How have you found this difficult?

✓	Feeling	How It Is Expressed
	Rejection	"Why don't you love me?"
	Betrayal	"How could you do this to me?"
	Despair	"It's over."
	Fear	"I will never be able to get through this."
	Guilt	"What is wrong with me? This is my fault."
	Shame	"I'm such a fool. Why didn't I see this coming?"
	Disgust	"You make me sick!"
	Anger	"I hate you for this!"
	Bitterness	"You will never hurt me again!"
	Revenge	"You will pay for this!"

4. Read 1 Peter 5:7. What is the basis for giving your "care" to God? Review the emotional responses you recorded above and commit each of these to God. Example: *"Lord, I feel so angry about _____ but I am giving this to you."* Memorize 1 Peter 5:7.

5. Read Isaiah 26:3. What does God promise to provide for the one whose mind is steadfast in its trust in God?

6. Memorize Proverbs 3:5–6.

Project 2: Getting Things Right with God

1. Read Psalm 139:23–24. Ask God to expose how you have sinned against him.

2. On a separate piece of paper, list the sins God brought to mind for which you are personally responsible. Be specific:

    (a) *What sins have been manifested in your attitude?* This may include bitterness, hostility, rage, selfishness, coldness, revenge, stubbornness, hatred, or self-righteousness.

    (b) *What sins have been manifested in your*

words? This may include things you have said about your spouse to others (gossip), or hurtful things you have said to your spouse to inflict pain (evil speaking).

(c) *What sins have been manifested in your actions?* This list may include actions you did that you should *not* have done, as well as actions you *did not do* that you should have done.

3. Begin at the top of the list and acknowledge each item to God as a sin against him. Example: *"Lord, I realize that my attitude of bitterness toward my husband is a sin against you. It is wrong and inexcusable. It grieves you, hurts my husband, and corrupts me. On the basis of Jesus's death on the cross, I ask you to forgive me for this."*

4. Read through the following passages of Scripture and answer each question about God's forgiveness:

    (a) 1 John 1:9. What is the promise for those who confess their sins? What does this passage say is the basis of God's forgiveness and cleansing?

    (b) Psalm 103:12. To what extent has God

removed your transgressions against him?

(c) Jeremiah 31:34. How does God's promise
not to remember your sin against you give
you hope?

(d) Micah 7:19. How does the picture of God
casting your sins into the sea reflect God's
compassion to you?

5. Thank God for his forgiveness and ask him to
help you live obediently in light of the grace he
has shown you.

Project 3: Waiting on God

What should you do as you wait on God to work
in your spouse's heart? The message of Psalm 27
provides some practical direction. Read the theme
of this psalm in verse 14.

1. *Cultivate your faith in God (vv. 1–3).* Faith in God
   is cultivated as we commit to looking to God in
   our trouble.

   (a) Read verses 1–3. How did David view God?
   What hope does this give you?

(b) Write a prayer to God expressing the truths from verses 1–3. Ask God to direct you because he is your light. Ask him to deliver you because he is your salvation. And ask him to defend you because he is your strength.

2. *Continue your fellowship with God (vv. 4–6).*

   (a) What was David's one main desire in verse 4?

   (b) How does seeking God above all else in times of trouble provide a sense of security (v. 5)?

   (c) In verse 6, David commits to worship. How might choosing to worship God, even in your trouble, change your perspective?

3. *Confess your failures to God (vv. 7–10).* Our deepest needs in life are due to sin.

   (a) What was David's greatest need in verses 7 and 9?

   (b) What was David's assurance when those closest to him abandoned him (v. 10)?

   (c) How does this encourage you in your situation?

4. *Commit your future to God (vv. 11–13).*

    (a) How was David's commitment to following God expressed in these verses?

    (b) In what ways are you following God right now?

Where Can I Get Further Help?

Harvey, Dave, *When Sinners Say "I Do": Discovering the Power of the Gospel for Marriage* (Wapwallopen, PA: Shepherd Press, 2007)

Jones, Robert D., *Restoring Your Broken Marriage: Healing after Adultery* (Greensboro, NC: New Growth Press, 2009)

Lane, Timothy S., *Forgiving Others: Joining Wisdom and Love* (Greensboro, NC: New Growth Press, 2004)

MacArthur, John F., *The Freedom and Power of Forgiveness* (Wheaton, IL: Crossway, 1998)

Sande, Ken, *The Peace Maker: A Biblical Guide to Resolving Personal Conflict* (Grand Rapids, MI: Baker, 2004)

Smith, Winston T., *Help! My Spouse Committed Adultery: First Steps for Dealing with Betrayal* (Greensboro, NC: New Growth Press, 2008)

Books in the *Help!* series include …

(More titles in preparation)